Rift
A
Collection of
Poems

Rift

A
Collection
Of Poems by
Steven Burns

2017

Copyright © 2017 by Steven Burns

All rights reserved. This book or any portion thereof may not be reproduced or used in any manner whatsoever without the express written permission of the publisher except for the use of brief quotations in a book review or scholarly journal.

First Printing: 2017

ISBN 978-1-9997620-0-1

Ste.burns@gmail.com

Dedication

A big thank you to my family. Who inspired and yes, helped edit this work. You all knew it was something I had to do and you gave your time freely in helping me to accomplish it.

Contents

Chocolate Coated Thunder 1
Dragons 3
Children 4
Family 5
Teacher 6
Parent 7
Walk 8
The Watcher 9
Modern Day Zombie 11
The Green Man 16
Moon 20
What's Wrong? 23
The Black Veil 24
Trapped 26
Hate 27
My Light 29
Denied 30
Need 31
Gone 33
Realisation 34
Problem Escaped 36

Succeed with Fear	38
Decide	39
Here	40
If you Need a Reason	41
Fallen	43
The Right Road	44
The New Religion	45
The Pause	47
Escape the Corner	49
Hanging in a Tree	54
No Threat	55
Conform or Reform.	56
Humans Unopened	57
To Tell	59
Nature's Notion	61
The Storm	63
Steal	64
Xmas	65
Autumn in the Trees	66
Summer in the Trees	67
Winter in the Trees	68
Add	69
Explain	70

Rift
A
Collection
Of Poems

Chocolate Coated Thunder

In this moment of chaos I hover,

        surrounded in blooming thunder.

As my joyous children plunder,

        ensconced in a world of wonder.

The wrappers they tear asunder,

        to reveal chocolate coated pleasure.

Their gnashers chomp on sweet tinder,

        stoking up on rocket sugar.

Dials say full, on they career,

        energy levels sear.

Giggle hertz increasing, frequency shocking,

        ears screaming, squeals brimming.

Sonic boom breached, climax reached,

        descending avalanche, fading and beached.

Brown war painted faces bemoan approaching flannel,

        as cave paintings are redacted from apparel.

Flame in tummy gutters as sleep starts to flutter,

        bed gently calls, in soothing murmur.

Dragons

As my children race

    around the lawn, chased

        by dragons of pink feather bowers crazed.

They lift their faces to the glare

    and stare

        at the vapour trail lying there

            created by the jetting roar of the

                serpent's maw.

There be dragons everywhere

    in the sky and under the stair

        the barbecue fire issues from their lair

        tendrils of smoke twist like snakes

        through the air.

The Wendy house on the lawn their only care.

Children

They are of us and not us.

They are connected to the thread,

> stretching back to the Rift.

They are not ours, they are theirs.

They need guidance, not our thoughts.

They need to shape their dreams, not live our life.

They need to make their mistakes, not perfect our story.

They need our time formed from love, not begrudged moments soaked in strife.

They are the future and our present colours their past

There is hope in them glowing, a beacon to the moths of reason.

Quiet your longing, enter the pool of reflection.

Child is questioning, seeing all colour – acceptance.

Family

For Acceptance, Mending, Internal Lies Yielded,

Automatic forgiveness of morals Lapsed,

Madness bred from Inclusion,

Ideals held and shared as Maxims,

Love, as the one pure Aggregate,

Your Love Is Magnified And Forever.

Teacher

The child stares, symbols tumble, this thought

  she cannot snare.

Attention flits, a butterfly in a field of flowers,

  she cannot sit.

The warm class, regimental rows facing forward,

  she cannot pass.

The concept abstract, fundamentally alien,

  she cannot extract.

She tries to ponder her teachers thunder.

She wonders if his face in the dark, actually glows red like embers.

Does volume increase comprehension? she sees no reason.

She needs a new pattern not the usual hammering.

Parent

To raise a child is the hardest thing.

To teach and nurture, without dousing their spark.

To give them choice, unbiased by your fears and desires.

To show them life, dark and light, without scarring them.

To protect them from themselves, even as they hate you.

To guide them with no pressure, to a path of their choosing.

To be there and at the same time not to be there, as they learn.

To keep them safe when they want to explore.

To let them go, when they want to stay.

To be a parent is to live in paradox.

Walk

As I walk, I am thinking.

I am thinking of my walk.

My walk is leading my thinking.

My thinking is of my walk.

As I walk, I am thinking.

Thinking of one foot in front of the other.

Pounding in rhythmic order.

Thinking in patterns circular.

Trudging to my destination or my origin.

Thinking of the beginning as I pass the ending.

As I walk, I am thinking.

The Watcher

The watcher sits and waits, contemplating fate.

Its role to stare, consume with eyes empty as desert skies.

Not to judge, simply to store all that's before.

To witness change, identify patterns within the infinite rays.

It sees humans seethe in uncontrolled expansion, petri dish of confusion.

Forming groups of no discernible difference, nations, states, families, religions, all human.

Wars break out, caused by ruler's dominance of group view, abstract cues.

Killing their cousins, blinded by the minute variance of genetics, dogmas and vision.

Their minds programmed by the promised unobtainable.

A single idea can save millions, while another destroys countless others.

Most days a replay, with some being seeds of exquisite memory.

The watcher sees the arc of human history, all hues hidden within the dark and the light.

It wonders, when will human's stop lying to themselves and grab the responsibility, the trust bequeathed by their home.

The universe's in multitude, an infinite spray of charm.

Their minds still echoing off the cavern walls enclosed in the valleys folds.

Be more like the watcher, audit nature's sonnets, ride in her power, take pleasure in the great and varied show.

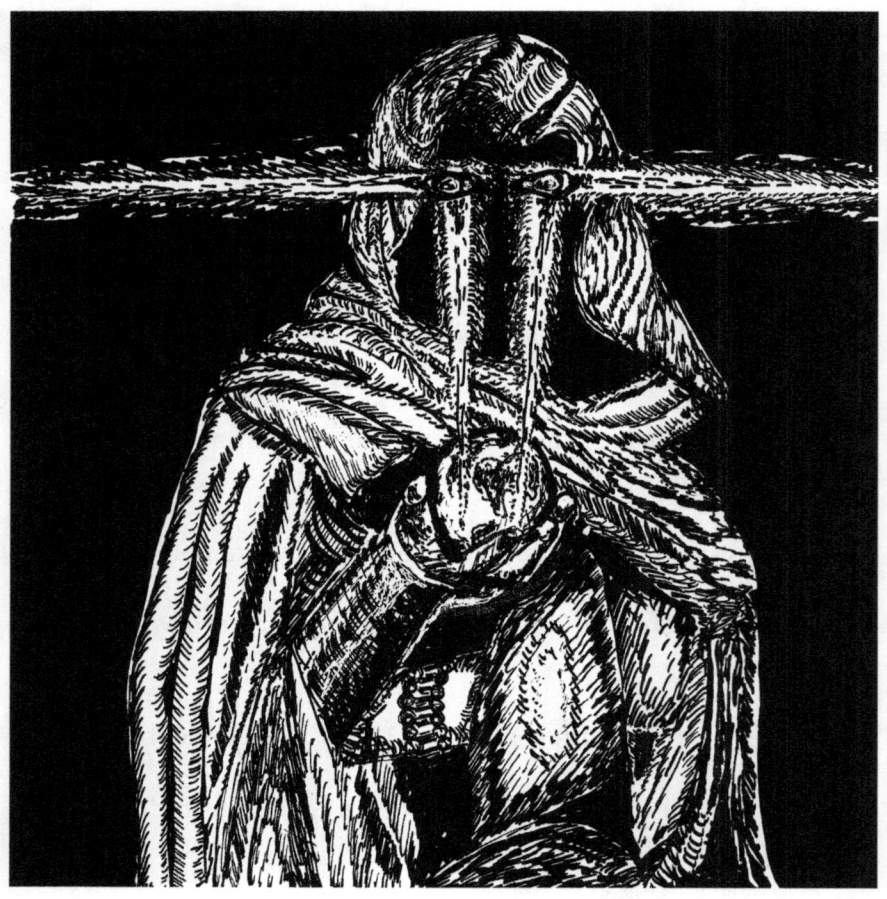

Modern Day Zombie

Modern day zombie.

Clutching his decay.

Soft blue interplay.

Casts pallid complexion.

Blank stare fixation.

Toxic screen insinuation.

Sustenance not found.

Re-cycled life abounds.

Phantom vibrations resound.

Alarm, must except.

Blinkered by precepts.

Narrowing this concept.

Horizon, turns corridor.

Options gone forevermore.

Path not sure.

Led by web

Trapped, spider fed.

Nothing but lead.

Clinging to decay.

No thought today.

Update profile, replay.

Tweet useless text.

Beauty everywhere, vexed.

Enticement provides hex.

Technology promised connection.

Instead, contact partition.

Disembodied word ocean.

Separated from caress.

Loves lips moistness.

Fingertip, glass lingers.

Through crystal screen.

The silent scream.

Stuck in dream.

In your view.

Not with you.

Attention no virtue.

Release the mirror.

Take the fervour.

Wipe the blur.

Modern day zombie.

Come out to play.

Throw phone away.

The Green Man

Within the yew, concealed from view, lichen crowned.

Leaves dance and play, serpentine lay, tendrils writhe and display.

An ancient face re-born, cast from heart wood, reformed.

Antlers grown shaped as roots age, worn and torn from clay.

Lids of bark open, displaying eyes of emerald knowing.

Ageless smile skits across the face, spider-like leaving no trace.

Flowing emotion animate features, flux of seasons holding reason.

The face is known before our sight, its song we sing as we scheme.

He asks, "who has woken me from my empty sleep?" no dreams for He.

"I am man," says man to He. He sighs storms through rotted boughs, decay.

"You are trouble to me, name and wall, waste and want, misery is your plea."

"I want it all, and I want it now. I will take it, strip you naked and watch you fall."

Face distorts as retort is framed, "Yes you will try" Oak breaking in storm "and you will die" snapped the reply.

"I am young, death holds no fear you crazy old tree. Why should I listen to you old and green?"

He shakes, needles fall, changing from green to brown as they hit the soft loomed ground, carpet bound, no sound.

The shaking grows violent as laughter issues from scar in turbulent gusts, reeking of musk holding dust.

"Why do you laugh? I will not be mocked. This is my world. It is mine to abuse and use, shape to my version of me."

"Really? Let us see!" As Ivy slowly unwraps and catches man's arms in a Jesus Christ pose, a marionette held aloft, controlled.

The face stares directly in to man's mind. Pictures race, connections trace, realities shown, no adornment known.

Man's mind screams as the truth is stripped. The models torn down, shown the splinter in the abyss. This is fear.

Man sees his actions amplified by the lens of humanity, mind narrowed burning and gouging this Earth, life unvalued.

Man hears the Oceans cry as rivers of poison his race exudes boil the seas dry.

Man smells the air, turn from sweet to bitter thick acrid stink, as nature's felled and exhumed for fuel.

The witness becomes the victim. Man starts to age, shedding youth's robes in fast decay, accelerated by his environment betrayed.

His bodies imperfections, evolutions second guessing, copied faults amassing, fed by own worldly actions.

Diseases and illness take root, cancers seek to consume as man's cry escalates.

Man's body wastes away with struggles and days, withering in the drought like the crops he planted in the deserts he created.

Man's mind wonders. No longer grasping of the moment, meandering in past fantasies.

Broken his strength fails. The Ivy releases the shell. Man sees it rot at the foot of the Yew feeding the aged tree.

Then Man is standing staring at the foliate head concealed in the bough of the Yew, bright eyes piercing.

"Do you see?" says He, in voice of history. "You and me are entwined just like my Ivy."

"Death and Life, just like Dark and Light, are needed by all for eternity. Should I fall, so will you. Man is nature and nature is Man."

Moon

As I lie napping in a transient state, my mind wondering through bleak landscape, in a land of void darkness draped.

There is a scratching, my circadian rhythm broken by metronomic tapping, emanating from skeletal hand rasping against my pane.

Dragged to realities shore, my dreams seem more real than this projected reel of room. This enhanced view moonlit slewed washed with metallic hues.

I drag myself out of pit, fighting against primitive instinct. Stumble across rug and dross towards my curtained fear, the source.

Straining to hear, listening to the universe. Suddenly the screech, opening of long buried coffin. Nails dragged over glass, teeth clenched breath past.

I reach out to pull the curtain, the picture revealing, sentinel trees, limb tortured grasping at my window opening.

Looking upon view, etched by borrowed light, washed over the silver shore lapping at my front door.

Realisation dawns, at moons rise. World bathed in foiled light shimmering real to dream, this ephemeral scheme.

No fear lies here, but wonder, watching the trees sway and murmur, dancing in this enchanted atmosphere.

My eyes lead to the silvered glistening grass, cresting and ebbing like a mercury sea, waiting for the wave to break at my door.

The metallic hills frame this vistas protagonist, glowing without a right, this lunatic's cue the sister to our light.

Her altered iridescence has shown my world's details in stannic tones. I hold no fear as I drink in this moment washed clean by lunar shine.

What's Wrong?

"What's wrong?" she says.

"Nothing," he replies.

Everything, he thinks.

Nothing but lies, staring at the sink, softly she cries.

Tears unseen, uneaten food, wrapped in cling film.

Packaged emotion, worm cocooned, his guts twisted.

Does he know, do I care, tears flow.

Bubbles clear, glass squeaks upended. Speak.

Nothing. Completes the emptiness, consigns the affair.

Pent tension, ripped sawed, freezing her despair.

Fridge opened, cold and light spill out, as he shelves the food.

The Black Veil

I am here, somewhere, in the hissing fizzing din within.

Wading through the everyday, fighting the static and delay.

Thoughts tumbling and aching, a well of worries descending.

Doubts distorting every sight, clamouring for life and fight.

The cold soup of my mind, squirming like eels in their tormented hell.

Trapped in a vortex of shards, mirrors of notions, mind lacerated hard.

Each one stinging, multiplying with bell-like ringing.

Pain physical, internal, external, eternal crashing like a tide.

Where am I in this raging ocean? chemical flotsam.

Faded clone awakes, stealing me away before daybreak.

The outline of me is eroded by woes, sand castle in waters throes.

Pick out the diamonds, the cold lucid seconds.

Separate the sprites from the spilled suns rays bright.

Tease from the foam and churn of mashed up musing, re-form.

Bring the wil-o'-the-wisp back into focus, wind the tendrils around the locus.

Weave the torments into being, pull through to the core my feelings.

Shed the black veil, the treacle mire that passes through my jail.

Wrap up and solidify my will, re-sculpt complete and still.

To escape from within, ponder the external, and wonder.

Create and shape your life, within this mould you will thrive.

Have a plan, an aim, set a goal to lighten your soul.

Love the people, whose lodestar smiles point the path for miles.

Keep on this course, but beware, the veil is always close to its source.

It is part of you, controlled and welcomed it can enhance this is true.

Learn that you are complete, a human, and that we all compete.

Remember we are war but what soothes our cares we all share.

Trapped

Her words were like a spider in a rose

beautiful

delicate

scented

cradling fear.

As she drew me near

Hate

'You are what you eat', the common expression states.

Every three months you are refreshed, sculpted remade.

Each cell copied, replaced, blueprinted from DNA to mirror you.

The only thing remaining is thoughts and memories stored.

So how can they say they do not belong?

If you eat, drink and breathe in one place for three.

You are made of that place so you see.

The only thing that makes you different from me,

are your thoughts and memory.

Hate is such a strong word we inform our children.

Do not use it lightly for it is deep, dark and loathsome,

it will creep like cancer, spread like rot and consume,

till all that remains is twisted thoughts and distorted wisdom.

The only shield against hate is to educate.

Teach the children we are but one animal all linked to the primary primate.

In generations we may exterminate this insidious weed.

If we fail, no more thought, only the world's dream will be our fate.

Mark this poem return to sender, for attention of Pandora.

In the dust the lion's head mane will remain.

Return to sender Pandora's folly.

My Light

In the darkness there's a light,

      a fiery beacon within my sight,

      a warm season within this blight.

This perfection is your right.

Denied

She plays like a child,

      enticing me to become wild.

She knows not what she holds,

      in hands so gentle they scold.

I wish I had been told,

      her power over me could leave me cold.

Need

Your face is an oasis for a lone traveller,

      a temptation for a priest,

         inspiration for a painter.

But for me, it's pain to behold.

Your body is a shrine for a pilgrim,

      an alter for a father,

         a muse for a sculptor.

But for me, it's pain to hold.

Your soul is a beacon for a sailor,

    a star for a seer,

    a sunset for a director.

But for me it's pain so cold.

Your mind is a path for a navigator,

    a mystery for a diviner,

    a passage for a conductor.

But for me, it's pain untold.

So why do I need you so?

Gone

To hold me she told me was cold.

As I had no heat to treat her with.

Her eyes have skies wrapped in lies.

No wonder I froze her as I rose forever.

For my eyes held scars not stars for her.

Realisation

Can I ask a question?

Can I expect devotion?

Can I worship at the grave of creation?

I don't need the ocean of tears,

I don't want the covered sneers,

I don't have time for people's fears,

I want people to care for nature's trust,

I want to show that not all age is rust,

I want power to ebb, fade, become just.

I think all are needed to overcome our plight,

I think every creed and gender is needed in this fight,

I think the only evils are faiths and values formed in mind's night,

I believe dreams can power the stars,

I believe daughters may be able to heal a man's scars,

I believe time will show all humanity, can be gods of their cures.

Problem Escaped

"I can't," the mantra of doubt.

Beats as pulse through self.

Encountered dread, implied.

Brain crashed.

Primal function invoked.

No thought, just fear congealing.

Idea big, gravity crushing.

Air too dense, ground tilting.

No opponent but the id.

Route blocked, emotion barred.

Escape senseless, as prison within.

Must grasp, idea stung.

Shown how illuminates way.

Help given, advice taken.

Original thought shaped and tempered.

"I can," the mantra of creation.

Succeed with Fear

Within is a silent storm, a puddle of fire.

Cold and burning gently engulfing.

It's gradually smearing me away.

Turning me into a background wash.

Definition, escaped life cascades on and over.

Sand trickles grain by grain I cannot grasp I haven't the heart to try.

Age just a number eroded by time corroded by the mundane.

Where is ambition, when life happens to others?

This poor watercolour tainted with tears needs vivid ink, a guided hand.

The hand can only be the authors, the colour an attitude.

The only thing you truly know is yourself, do not be self-blind.

Locate a single truth, make it your first anchor.

Learn to fail with ease and succeed with fear.

Decide

Within the spin, whirling thoughts, cogs scream.

Rushed life crushes, dreams gutter, no colour.

Standing still falling, heart stutters, emotion shuttered.

Hold onto self, being coalesced, world focused.

Anchored to present, time gifted, slowed season.

Fail with grace, expel fear, path determined.

Here

Life is motion,

      constant agitation buffeted by numerous needs.

Primitive notion,

      controlling reaction against these fears.

Demon concoction,

      trapping our emotion blinding our escape.

Need to find your centre,

      steady the creature make it your steed.

Inhale the wonder,

      exhale your doubts, drop your shoulders ride high.

Learn you are apart and one with everyone,

      stand and shout I am HERE.

If you Need a Reason...

Often life seems hard, cold and frozen.

"Why won't it work?" you mutter as you struggle in the task.

    Then the word fair creeps up and fills you with despair.

Treat fair with caution.

The universe does not function to enable you to flourish.

    It does not care about fair and neither should you.

If you want something to happen.

Make it so, coax the problem, shape it to fit the solution.

    Effort is always needed, energy and passion.

To convert normal to sublime.

Add a little bit more, chip a sliver from your soul.

    Elevate your work incrementally, create a smile.

This extra spice will go forward.

Pushing the boundary just a bit every day with a flourish.

    Creates an elevator for everyone.

        Is this not fair?

Fallen

Look upon me

and hold me in vision

Cradle me

and hold me in blindness.

I am the light which fell,

you are the ground which consumed.

I am part of you, the basic start.

You are part of me the ultimate end.

The Right Road

Round and round I go,

as emotions drip off my brow,

a snarl slowly coils my maw,

as BMW's arse flashes red,

machine's belching out dread,

as I fight through arteries blocked and bled,

my heart pushes pollution through,

the engine pounds our witches brew,

the world is given a grey hue,

as I grope towards my end,

I reach a road that never bends,

and find a light that transcends.

The New Religion

Every day an injury, a tiny wound caused by a stranger.

A thorn inserted into your mind, a splinter.

A belief shredded by a cheap chat show, cut up by someone heading home.

Art downgraded to a footnote, culture watches banality designed to be reality

Whistle blower shows the truth then condemned and denigrated by MP and troll.

A present delivered to the people, wrapped in Panama Papers smoking like a macerated cigar.

Lies told to control, incite people to war. Even the Lord of Flies silk tongue would find it difficult to turn so much scorn.

Jobs in drought as the river flows east, rising to the sun. Dragging the driftwood of dreams behind to be junked by the great tsunami of souls.

Row by row, all you know is twisted and gnawed by the rats who blow -

hot and cold dollops of misery shined and preened marketed for your delight.

Open your gullet and swallow life's canned tripe. Pretend it tastes like freedom that you once believed in.

No longer individuals, just nodes in this sea of economy. This market of wool bearing animals.

Imprisoned by enforced desires, wants imprinted on mind - moulded by unobtainable goals, always wanting more.

Gradually de-sensitised to pain suffered by others as we drown in our insipid sea of loneliness.

Standing upon the unfortunate, grasping with no care, plying any deceit just to snare that new shinny treat.

Knowing the right but fearing the fight, as nature faces our undeniable plight.

Bit parts in this machine, all we can be, stripped away, left with pure consumerism, the new religion.

All hail neo-liberalism.

The Pause

One of life's hardest lessons is the pause,

This may seem trite or even implausible,

To pause for some is simply impossible.

Let me explain this error of human endeavour,

Tasks and thoughts like parasites clamour for our favour,

We find it hard to grasp the pause as it turns to vapour.

The pause is vital and insightful.

Wise men and shamans have promoted it through the ages.

They have described it as meditation and prayer, but it's a pause and this is fair.

In this mental state of trance,

Life simply stalls and reality falls,

It is into this space created, heaven is called.

So next time you see a child awake and yet dreaming, leave them be,

They know the charm of the pause, you see,

Learn the cause and…

Escape the Corner

It's hard to remember the burning ember

    everyday possibilities new

        waiting for life's tinder.

The secrets cue and slowly reveal

    one after another

        merging together a kaleidoscopic view.

Life continues to snowball

    rushing through chapters

        gathering grey mundane wrappers.

It's tough to suckle the child

    free it from the punished corner

        show it the world's wonder.

The lesson is not taught

    the hushed whispers

        stand grey in mind's cellars.

The dog is baying

    at the leashed child

        as hope is defiled.

These turbulent thoughts swirl

    created from observed fakes

        founded in media's glossy heart-breaks.

Path trampled by numerous feet

    Dante's vision within

        falling through his rings.

Caterpillar cocooned in worries

    no butterfly to exhume

        only the internal gloom.

Mind insulated from body

    no one sure of the link

        but all feel the brink.

Cast a light into the well

    unveil the child's eyes

        look into your truth, crystallized.

Free the promise you were

    waken life's mission

        traverse your new dominion.

Be wary of the everyday

    normality and buts

        trapped in the same old ruts.

Enemies come in comparison

    me to you

        invasions of doubts accrue.

Emotions can poison

    render your dark interior

        stage set for failure.

Fight these gnawing worms

    with the gift's you know

        deeds not started, yet to sow.

Catch the old child's smile

    the one used to greet the new

        place it on full view.

Charge into that crazy dream

    forget static regret

        laugh and scream to the final sunset.

Hanging in a Tree

Where is the value in two husks hanging from a tree.

Once they were being's, holders of dreams.

Now they are empty sacs without seams.

Maybe a sign sighing in the wind, a warning of male schemes.

This act shocking yet mundane in this ancient barren custom.

Thousands of years embraced ideals that separate and excuse ill.

Levels of social cast enforced, believed to be divine law.

Simply an excuse to let the monster loose.

Throw away your humanity, enter guilt-free this orgy.

Modern law still in its thrall, victims swing.

We are told by their own hand they hang.

Two girl's close cousins, related to all, relieved they fall.

Men confess to the barbarous act, the vessels broken, sullied mean nothing.

Small flames snuffed before they blazed never to light this world.

Still the darkness is allowed to walk free, as they died at their own decree.

No Threat

Lying in bed feeling the tide creep.

Listening to the house deform as its weight settles.

Mind staggers through memories faded.

Each experience singed by the present.

Family segregated in their individual stupors

My own heartbeat a giant's footstep, shakes.

Adrenaline is in vain sweat on brow, trapped.

Where is the threat?

Always the passenger, just out of reach, a dark breach.

The crack is always there our initial scream echoes -

until it returns as our final gasp.

The threat is real, the cure I'm not sure, but it may lay next door.

Or possibly these words I write, may well echo past my night.

Conform or Reform.

Packaged into class, set in rows.

We all stare at the product as it crows.

Syllabus chosen of average truth told in preachers throws.

All set to accomplish mundane tasks.

However hard we ask nothing ever gets passed

Our attention has been wilted by every stilted word cast.

All thirty treated the same all thirsty for originality.

Then released into the world penned as sheep in our own thoughts.

Wanting release but lost from the doors.

Screaming as we sleep at the passage of youth.

The funnels aperture narrows to the grave.

As we are pulled through life clinging to salvation in isolation.

Humans Unopened

Born a boy, baby opened to life shaded with male vision.

Unknown the flip side not even recognised or given thought.

Not even blinkered just not realised the other side of the gap.

As I continue through my life my biases are preordained manhood understood.

I am hu-Man, I can do anything I want there is no mould for me.

Until the act of union creates a small loud ripple in my views reality.

I stare into the red pruned screaming face of daughter under compact florescent glare.

The world screeches around me deforming as my eyes re-focus and settle on her.

Now I listen to words spoken and videos streamed containing dangers unseen before.

Reassessing the created pain for the fairer gender that has always been.

Of glass ceilings and multiple rapes,

of food disorders and stolen sexual rights,

genital mutilation and domestic violence,

the minute differences without even realising,

boys are faster stronger and cleverer

this statement not muttered but implied by multinationals trying to flog coloured plastic

girls get the dolls the cute talking animals, boys get the tech and the weapons.

girls of five are emblazoned with pink sexual innuendo

while boys get to think while playing with their lego.

How do I encourage growth from girl to woman instilling strength in self -

while fighting the machine of the divided world pigeon-holing my girls?

Need to teach the keys, the states of mind to be independent without breaking their sense of themselves.

Being a father to daughters opens you up.

You see the other side and how it bumps and slides along the masculine world.

Supporting while being used by humans unopened.

To Tell

I try to speak,

    to tell,

    to still my heart.

But it's hard to speak

    to tell

    to still my heart.

Her beauty provokes, it holds

    it snares

    it takes my air.

I cannot escape, its hold

    its snare

    it takes my air.

I need release, her power

        her air

        her aura a cell

My mind a prisoner in her stare.

Nature's Notion

Embraced by kaleidoscope greens and gleams

    flowing in verdant streams.

The wind conducting the harmony

    boughs sway while leaves play.

Dancing flares partnered with emerald flame

    projecting their show, on the ground below.

Blackbirds vanity rippling through the canopy

    notes mingling with others changing tonal colours.

Insects hover, passing in and out of vision

    sun creates, shadows delete.

Butterflies flutter by, landing to warm then continuing on

    following their quest nectar seeking.

I lie cradled in wind's sigh, small in the green

    heart beating keen.

Life ebbs and slows in time with breeze and boughs

    as I doze beneath the pastoral ocean.

Lost but found in nature's notion.

The Storm

The wind hurls itself against my home.

Tendrils of air whip and search for ingress to my lair.

Safe I believe myself to be, warm, content and free.

The storm cannot touch me.

This image is false, man's storm is yet to be born.

Bombs and guns do not care, whose soul they snare.

Guided to truth, funnelled by ideals, corralled and free.

The storm has entered all.

Steal

Steal away with me,

    witness the world with child-eyed zeal.

Feel the tender breeze,

    caress through lover's fingers heal.

Trace our path on,

    futures unborn waiting, wanting to reveal.

Xmas

Celebrate today ordered by tradition distorted and stolen.

Forced to happiness, religious ideology drowned in material blasphemy.

No belief I hold, none needed.

Surrounded by pools of laughter, spells of daughter's creation.

Wife's smiles illuminated by dancing flame.

Drink in hand, warm within, time to be, caught in family.

Cheers...

Autumn in the Trees

Sitting in the shifting sun, while clouds scud along.

Enjoying the last hesitant heat this November's last treat.

Every dilation of sun, gives a sigh of breath a constant beat.

Each breath causes a small shudder, leaves fall, another small surrender.

Flaming colours pile under the gentle swaying boughs.

Mourning are the trees for the loss of the sun.

Sacrificing their coats as the last rays torch their crowns.

Summer in the Trees

Short the shadow, cool and thin.

Sun peaking.

Heat of noon, keen and thick.

Shade reviving.

Sat by tree, thick and cool.

Held napping.

Dream of love, keen and slim.

Tree spreading.

Winter in the Trees

Bone dry, ice cold crystals spread.

Over the skeletal hand, structures reaching for the sun.

Growing with no life stuck to dormant vigour.

Their precise beauty mathematician's lament.

As they creep along nature's lungs fracturing light.

Building their form from geometric norms.

White and pure angular repetitions clamour.

Climbing over one another dancing to the frost.

Add

I cannot see the end of me,

I cannot see the start of me,

I can only see what is before me,

I cannot stop the death of me,

I cannot stop the start of me,

I can only stop the fear held in me,

I cannot light the dark before me,

I cannot light the dark after me,

I can only shine a light on the truth of me,

Maybe I can learn from behind me,

Maybe I can inform the future passed on from me,

Hopefully I can add to the bloom from me.

Explain

Concept explained,

face close,

as breath mixes,

eyes holding mine

searching for a glimmer.

Still mind mudded,

abstract figures stuck in congealed crud, unmoving.

I stare at the paper,

the headlights to my rabbit brain,

caught in the beam of uncertainty.

Taught the blocks,

but mind struggling with the construction,

searching for the key.

www.ingramcontent.com/pod-product-compliance
Lightning Source LLC
Chambersburg PA
CBHW071741040426
42446CB00012B/2417